HEART OF AN
INDIGO CHILD

Dedication

Willie T. Hall Jr., Daddy, this book is in dedication to you. I remember you telling me how much of a great writer you have been in your life. That in itself enlightened me to just what kind of man you are. Having that in common with you has such gravity that pulls to my heart. I am so proud to be your baby girl. I love you.

Psalm 139:13-16 (NLT)

*13 You made all the delicate, inner parts of my body
and knit me together in my mother's womb.
14 Thank you for making me so wonderfully complex!
Your workmanship is marvelous—how well I know it.
15 You watched me as I was being formed in utter
seclusion,
as I was woven together in the dark of the womb.
16 You saw me before I was born.
Every day of my life was recorded in your book.
Every moment was laid out
before a single day had passed.*

About the Author

Stacy Lynn Wylie was born Stacy Lynn Hall in Cincinnati, OH on June 30, 1981. She has been writing since she was about 8 years old. She is a US Veteran having served 12 years honorably in the United States Air Force. She is a married mother of 6 children including two stepsons. She is also a recent college graduate and a Master Cosmetologist.

She began reciting her poetry publically in 2008 under the stage name "Black Herstory." In 2011, she adopted the stage name "SHE"- now known on the spoken word circuit as the Indigo Child "SHE".

Her notable performances include "Emmett Till's Death"-published by the Lackland Air Force Base Talespinner, "Look"-spotlighted by UBNG(Urban Nights Poetry Group) CEO, Garry Miles for the Martin Luther King Jr. "I Have a Dream Too" tribute and "Conversation" in dedication to the memory Malcolm X and Black History month 2009. She has competed in spoken word competitions in which she has always garnered first place. The cities of competition include: San Antonio, TX; Fort Sam Houston, TX; Macon, GA; and Atlanta, GA. She also has opened for R&B artist, Chico DeBarge.

Acknowledgements

I can only say this it would not be possible if I hadn't been motivated my entire life by the people who believed in me the most.

First, Mommy and Daddy, I remember when my poetry was displayed in the form of "Hip Hop" and I was going to be the best rapper ever. Not best female rapper, but greatest of all time. You made me center myself and I am so grateful that you did. Mommy, you came with me to my first rap contest and I feel I won 1st place because I listened to you and toned down my demeanor to be me. I dressed very nice instead of a typical rap artist like the others. I went on stage and wrecked shop by just being me. I have carried that with me in life. Trying to always be the best in what I am doing. Magnifying my individuality is what you and Daddy taught me my whole life and I am forever grateful to be raised by such wisdom, discipline, love, and confidence. Daddy, you are the greatest man I know. You are everything a man should be for and to his children. You never left us to worry about anything. Everything we needed in life you provided with love, consistency, and patience. Of course it may not have seemed that way to you, but as your child I never saw you break a sweat to give us the absolute best or close to best in life. I cherish you as a father and I am so grateful to have a chance to let you read the words of your baby girl in raw form. I love you, greatly.

Michael, my big brother...my ROCK...my friend...you are the absolute best brother in the world. I can't think of a time where you didn't have my back right or wrong...If I needed you 4am 5 hrs. away you would be on your way...no questions...the questions would come when you got to me(smile)...I learned everything of the art to and for words from you...I know I used to steal your work and pass it off as my own when I was like 8...but in the end you were flattered...not upset. You know... I wrote the best when I was in your old room...on that red comforter...I love you....Ericka Nichole...I can write a whole page to tell you how much I love you...all we have been through...all I will say is when your nephews and nieces get to bickering I tell them how it is to be a big brother or big sister based off the awesome big sister you were/are to me...every sport I played it was right behind you...when I decided to go to the Air Force it was because you were in the Navy and you told me to...now I have graduated from Master Cosmetology School preparing for Barbering School because you told me it was in me and I could do it...like YOU ALREADY HAVE...you never lead me wrong...you always push me...I've learned so much from you and I love you with all my heart

To my familee, Big Mom, Aunt Dorothy, Aunt Mildred, Uncle Sam, Shauna, Uncle Phil, Aunt Judy, Aunt Michael Rene, Aunt Shelli, Margie, Aunt Kim, Aunt Marilyn, Aunt Lisa, Uncle Aaron, Uncle Steve, Uncle Mike, The Pullins Family, The Rousseau Family, The Hall Family, The Wylie Family, The Mackey Family, The Magruder Family, The Stallworth Family, The Badger Family, My Chicago family, My Detroit Family, My St. Louis Family, My New York family, My New Jersey Family, I love you all dearly and thank you so much for your unwavering support!

To my best friends, Tonika, Kendra, and Regina-I love you and thank you for always supporting and believing in me for the last 20 years. Thank you for all the pep talks, the you know better talks, the deep heart to hearts, and the overall support whenever I have needed you. You will always be my SLIKS...

To my best sister-friends Lisa(Dodds), Tifney T., Lachelle, Tiyana(Pimpn), Deborah, Bianca A.,Toyia Tiffany, Nikki, Fatima, Autumn, Kidada, April, Carla, Deanna, Jenniefer, Mwangi, Renata, LaToya(Sissy),Asia, Sakina, Monique, Anna, Thaise, Allana, Jenny-I love you all, immensely and my life has been enriched by having you be a part of it...Thank you for showing up for me...

To my lil bro Victor- Chin up always...I am so proud of you and thank you for believing in me since DAY ONE- I love you!

Garry Miles and Nicholas Kendrick- I really don't know when I surrendered my fears to hear the ideas of your dreams in which you had for ME. It overwhelms me, never leaves me, and I will always be also known as the "Black Herstorian" because of you two. The platform you set up allowed all of us artists a place to leave it all on the stage if we needed to. I will be your UBNG princess/sister, forever and always. I love you two so much.

Deon Borden- I appreciate you putting the flame to my tail to get my words out to the world. You have been motivating me since we were kids and you popped back up after 20 years doing what you have always done. You reminded me of whom I forgot I was and I appreciate that more than words or actions can express. I love you, friend!

J. Faulkner-Who knew you were such the good friend? (smile)Thank you for supporting me, uplifting me with your words of encouragement, and reminding to keep the faith and be positive in all areas of my life...I sure appreciate the swift support and check ins just to make sure I'm staying encouraged and confident with my goals in spoken word... Love ya bighead!

To all of my family and friends who I am connected to through Facebook,(and I mean all of you) I want to say thank you for your overwhelming support and love through all my spoken word endeavors. You all have no idea to which the magnitude you have inspired and motivated me to do what I know and love to do best. Thank you so much for your consistent and unwavering support. I love you! Each one of you knows who you are to me, own this gratitude I am sending to you. Thank you!

To my NCH Family Class of 98, Class of 2000, Class of 2001, Class of 2002 and THE GREATEST Class of 99...It is so many of you to name, just know I take no words of encouragement lightly and I have a very good memory...I love you all very much!-

My Lady Trojans Basketball Team aka The Finest Team in the MVC, Coach Gregory Moore and Janine Johnson-I love you guys!

To the teachers who have helped my journey through life directly and indirectly- Mrs. Bauer, Mrs. Geibel, Mrs. DeGraffenreid, Mrs. Clyburn, Mr. Baarendsee, Mr. Kemphaus, Mr.Theado, Ms. Brown, Mr.Koeniger, R.I.P. Mrs. Sari-I always wished my children get as lucky as I was to have at least someone like one of you to be one of their educators! Thank you!!

Mrs. Leslie Davenport- I know I have always told you, you changed my life. It is because you did. I have never forgotten the key elements in keeping my sanity from day to day. Your level of devotion and faith is immovable, unshakable hence reassuring my faith in what I am capable of. I love you!

To Mrs. Eison- I hold you responsible to all I thought was impossible...my greatest deal of respect is to you...thank you for taking me under your wing and into your heart...you made some unbearable days bearable for me in those halls of NCH-I love you!!

My Virginia College Family- Thank you to all the staff/ instructors/ PD's for your support and dedication to the student body as a whole! I applaud the experience and am extremely grateful.

Dean Scott- I appreciate the enthusiasm and realness you provided to my experience at Virginia College as a whole. You were always easy to approach and provided encouragement and understanding with even more ease...Thank you for everything!

Ms. Robinson- Thank you for allowing a platform in which I was able to express a different form of my art...I appreciate your guidance throughout my tenure in Cosmetology!

To six people I could never forget if I tried...thank you for putting up with me...us artists tend to be a little insane and I was enriched to have gone crazy with you...

> Raychanda,-Renowned Perfectionist
> Crystal- Courageous Contender
> Krystalynn- Kaleidoscopic Dreamer
> Robert- The Revolutionary Duke
> Courtney-Constant Collaboration
> Ebony-Elephantine Creator

This is the way you present who you are, to me. I embrace each of you for your individuality and I hope you always remain that way! I love you!

Ms. Muhammad, Ms. Aziz, Ms. Brown, Mr. McClendon-It isn't how you changed my life...it was how I watched you make it point to change the life of others...and that kind of love and devotion cannot be taught...Ms. Montford-thank you for allowing me to bless your establishment with my poetic flow as it helped establish my base of people to touch with my craft. To the underclassmen in Master Cosmetology finishing in 2015 stay focused and be creative. Let nothing say your name like your work. I love you all!!!!

Lastly, I send my tidal wave support to the following organizations/individuals: Brown Girl Collective- thank you for the feature on your social network and the radio interview that allowed me to express my work of art to all who would listen-Marcie Thomas, CEO you are the bomb.com(smile) I appreciate you greatly and hold you responsible for the towering support to my FB poet page as it reached its most through your support and advertisement of my skill...God bless...

L.A.D.Y. Terra Denise- You are a gem, my dear. Remember we shared that ride from the Columbus airport as young Airmen in 2000. Well its symbolic...we are heading to the same place...making a difference in the world. You are a phenomenal example to all women and I wish you the greatest success so many generations can benefit from your empowerment. Love you girl!

YO- Yolanda Lattimore& Sincere -Thank you for each and every opportunity to participate on your platform. The love you have shown me since my arrival to GA has been nothing short of amazing. I wish you the greatest of things the world has to offer! Love you!

To my Guardian Angels:

Joi Nichole, Big Bob, Uncle Granville, Uncle Gene, Mitzi, James, Demetrius Wood, Nana, Grandma Holmes, Grandma Blair, Grandma Suzie, Grandpa Holmes, Grandpa Stallworth Grandpa Blair, Gail, Grandpa Kissy, Uncle Mike, Aunt Eithel "Annie", Uncle Vernon-I wasn't sure where my strength was coming from lately...now I know. Rest In Heaven. Everything I am, consists of bits and pieces from you all. You are in my heart and consistently stay in my dreams...crossing plains to be with me when I need it most...I love and miss you. I walk in the faith that one day we shall be reunited again.

To my Husband:

Ezra, words are not your form of communication, because people can say anything. And I know that you are a man of your word through action. So I appreciate you understanding my desire to creatively express myself every chance I get. The emotion between us has led to some of the most intense performances of my life. I love you, I appreciate you, and I hope you enjoy seeing my words in print.

To my Children:

Kenny, Ezra Jr. Jakalah, Jakobe, Elias, and Lyric-The conviction, the drive, the love, the realness of my words is stemmed from the joy already in my soul to have the most amazing children in my life. I am rich because of you. I am whole because of you. Everything great about me is because it's even greater about you. Anything you want in this world is attainable. Work harder, want harder, love harder and you will reach heights you never knew you could. I love you all so very much and I am SO proud of each and every one of you in unimaginable ways.

To my Nieces:

Ciera, Ashley, Daviana, Ci-Ci, Tyra, Ebony, Laurynn, Erynn,Taylor, and Rene'- I always hoped I would be able to inspire you. Motivate you. Encourage you. I hope after reading my words that I have. You all are beautiful young women. You are very smart and articulate. You are fueled with a desire to succeed naturally so simply put you got it...go get it! I love you all very much.

To my Nephews:

Markel, Marcel, and Jaden

Marcel and Jaden-stay focused, work hard, be mega in every sense of the word. I remember when you two were little boys with mischievous grins but big hearts. I wish I could have had more time for you two to get to know the artistic side of your Auntie, but it's okay. You will find out now. I love you two!

Markel, I have a feeling one day you and I will collaborate on something dynamic. You are such an artist with insane capabilities. Yes, your auntie is looking, watching, and observing. We are closer than you may suspect. Stay focused young man. I loved you since the day your mother carried you in my life. I was 17 and had no idea what real love was. But when I saw the look shared between you and my sister...I found out. I love you, nephew!

Contributors to this Book

My life changed the day President James Sutton told me my poetry was worthy of a publication and he could help make that happen. As a phenomenal author of the books ` 'Look at Your Boss! Rehabilitation for Your Career'-'Effective Leaders Mentor People and Manage Processes' and recently published 'BElieve in YOUrself",~ You made it so easy to take that leap of faith in a world where dreams are sold with no true effort to progress. My words now have a life on these bonded slices of tree and for that I will always respect you, be thankful to you, and support others as you have done for me. Thank you!!!!!

Table of Contents

Politically Correct

I'm so blessed, amazing, majestic, spirited, humbled, symmetrically intertwined with humility, sensitivity with my melanin based skin...a sterile heart within because I am black...onyx...gorgeous charcoal with the love of GOD penetrated through my bones into my soul...DAMN...being black is the best gift I never asked for...enriched with the love and admiration I have for my creator because I was born black ...and to no other races am I showing disrespect I won't say African-American to be politically correct...I am black...considering it's not a skin color or ethnic origin but more of a socially based racial classification related to institutionalized slavery...in turn made my ancestors in a constant battle to show the quality of their stature...I am black...solidified in a stirring way...though referred to in the dictionary as the opposite of good but the words are only visible in the most important literature because they are printed in black...standing out in a crowd...remarkably proud to be black...no mistake on my roots...my kinky hair and full lips...my mahogany tone...the implication of my cheekbones...I'm black...and I love it...

POPE

a wordsmith, creative imagery is my specialty so please grab a seat and close your eyes with me...inspiration is the canvass of my most intriguing autobiography as I remember the lessons in class where we were only taught half the truth...I saw why some educators taught chemistry instead of history because if you look deep into its ancestry the beautiful black skin you own is responsible for the most victories...and I...want to leap...high above the clouds every morning I awake to my journey...and I...want to seek out the hidden roots so I can truly understand the depths of me...do you? Or will it always be in the corner of our minds limited to an inch that there is truth and shame by the letter from Willie lynch...that's why...I would edge my cursive script into a notebook real thick so when my children are snooping through my room for something else they will find it...and read...feel their minds with knowledge as opposed to pornography...and my girls will join the learning pack instead of the one to experience teenage pregnancy...see I...vowed to never limit my frontal lobe to mediocrity and I...relive my mistakes daily when I dream of holding my second born while she was still warm but not a heartbeat...I am far from perfect...questioning the true meaning to liberal submission...but who am I? To challenge even a mere inkling from GOD...that's a constant reminder of falling short...but there is no sin for self-realization to encompass more...that's why...I have endured life's trauma...developing through adolescence from the prayers of my great grand mamas...mistaken often in the climax of my aerodynamic pieces is I am self-centered...not poetry pioneer ...but racist...not bold and cavalier ...but self-righteous...and that's the furthest from the truth... "I fight so hard in myself to be normal...but I was made to be fearless, courageous, I was made to dominate over negativity and rise to the enemy's occasion. I was made to be a warrior...showing up with him by my side to conquer battlefields and send weeds of hindrance to a place of consistent, non-existent...existence! I was made to be amazing and not settle for anything less than what I was created to obtain in life...he made me, knit me together in my mother's womb. Every stitch affiliated with success and happiness...I wasn't made to be normal...I was made to be GREAT....and so were you."

Watch

You watched me...Remaining vigilant....as for protection or safe keeping...devotional purposes to look or wait attentively and expectantly...expecting action... not foreseeing progress...expecting to see.....nothing...expecting to see a ghoulish creature with intent to cause harm...the hood...making the face darker than normal because I really was only a few shades richer...than you...my watcher...yet I diminished into the air wings swept to lift my spirit upwards and the only thing left is the verb that is intended to not relay with action of the body...just vision from the organs that detect light and convert it into electro-chemical impulses in neurons...do nothing but detect whether the surroundings are light or dark which is sufficient for the entrainment of circadian rhythms...the eyes...needing no actions...just the eyes...instead of seeing...and believing in better....for me...you saw a threat...either a threat to your life or a threat to your existence...and even as I am gone I want the truth to ring "All progress is precarious and the solution of one problem brings us face to face with something else" words of Dr. King...you watched me...as if you could never see me bringing an end to world hate...as if you could never see me picking up a scalpel to save a life...as if you could never see me educating your grandchildren...as if you could never see me in the highlights of NBA live...yet you still watched me....waiting to bring forth my fatality...as if I held no future you watched and eluded I was a menace to your society...like I didn't deserve the time to find my area of study to get a degree, masters ,or PHD...you watched me...distastefully...approaching me the way little kids describe being ran up on by a bully...and sadly...6 women didn't agree...the prosecutors weren't passionate enough to explain...that you didn't watch to see me or what I could be...but to see how much force you needed to hurt and consequentially murder me...and what seems so puzzling is me being just as you...a minority...generalizing that progress is the attraction that moves humanity...that was proven not to be true in this instance and I will be sure to let Marcus Garvey know...when I see him...Thanks to you I will meet Medgar Evers...George Washington Carver...Jackie Robinson...Coretta Scott King...Ossie Davis and Malcolm X... thanks to you I bring new meaning to a hoodie and being black...pivotal yet standing still...as I dance on God's soft matter anticipating a formal introduction to Emmett Till...then I will...

get to hear the perplexities of the race driven case that left a mask of hate on a lot of America's face...My halo...incased around the top of my head with no gravity...making requests to bless my family as they recover from having to so early put me to rest...thanks to you I will never be a dad...you watched me so intricately and yet it never crossed your mind I hadn't truly lived...thanks to you...my moms and pops will relive that catastrophic moment that took me away from them...and as I watch them so tenderly awaiting my moment to greet them again in heaven...what is your life like...oh that's right...got CNN following your traffic stops... your side chick...trips to the gun shop...ya fan base happy you got rid of another black face...the demise of your marriage and your wife's perjury...her fear of you as a result to your domestic battery...thanks to you...I'm gone...and thanks to me you are the newest kind of celebrity....

I will let you rest

I have let the omnipotent enter my life, my soul, my spirit and all that's kindred so one day I can see you again...the holiest place, the paradise, in this exceptional case I feel God was giving you samples of heaven even before you took your last breath...divinity, goodness, faith...along with various other virtues, rights belief or simply the will of God has let you finally rest...in peace...that doctrine that there is something divine, something of God in the human soul...I know to be true...the heavy belief our heavenly father smiled with a ray of sun when he decided to come get you...the ultimate book reads "I am the light of the world. Whoever follows me will never walk in darkness, but will have the light of life" and your transition hurts the root of my being...but in my heart there is a huge triumph...the permanent cessation of all biological functions that sustain a living organism...is what has become of your flesh...yet your spirit stays incased with each ripple of wind, each current in raging waters, and every sunset in Chicago that has settled on the lake...what has manifested in your departure has been made over for your arrival... I cried in disbelief and then prayed and believed you are in the condition of supreme happiness and peace while being absolutely pain free...smiling remarkably with all your gold teeth...to be absent from the body...is to be present with the Lord...so Uncle Gene...you will be missed... But I know God and his angels will forever keep you in bliss... I can warmly say without any burdens on my chest...God said it was time...so I will let you rest

Halo

I absolutely without a doubt...love you...the capacity you have to move vibrantly with my anatomy...so smooth, yet gentle...passive...then aggressive...I adore you...all that you stand for defies gravity and scientifically I wonder how you even exist...a Disney film had you sewn on for monogamous companionship...but I let you roam free...I await to withstand that pleasure of the double threat we expose and the dependability of the caliber in which embodies us is without words...you are amazing...direct light from the sun's direct source cannot reach due to obstruction by an object...it occupies all of the space behind an opaque stature with light in front of it...the two dimensional silhouette or reverse projection of me blocking the light allows you to be born...an astronomical object casts human-visible shadows when it's apparent magnitude is equal or lower that -4 between us...so I stand hand in hand with you through rays of sun...beams of the moon...and in the right conditions...the planet Venus...my admiration from you has been confirmed with many tests and subjects...and I adore you through the most meticulous kind of passion...at every light moment the anticipation of your arrival has me head over heels with Joi as I await...I hate the dark...darkness...as polar to brightness...is the absence of visible light...the appearance of black in a colored space...emotionally my response has metaphorical connotations...and so it is wrenching the pit of my gut because darkness completely separates us...and in the late fall of every year an hour is compromised....makes me wait longer to bounce through the rhythm of life with you and the light...what I will forever be grateful for will as follows...it is believed and therefore to me positively received...an alternate construct which shadows are in fact a representation of God's presence around an object...like a halo...so the next time it gets extremely opaque...I won't be angry...God conquers all...so soon enough I will dance with my shadow in his light again...

Gladiator

I know a gladiator...brave...uncompromised spiritually...ambition lines the inner walls of his heart muscle...a champion...he won't sell his soul for freedom or be oppressed my societal bleeding of his being to be ideal I know a gladiator...he left a life seeking hood credibility to adapt to this world and offer it some grown man integrity......solid as an oak tree ...transformed his name from his arrests warrants to a college degree...I know a gladiator...with visions that became dreams...individuals that became teams...revolutionary as band of brothers...not glorifying gang affiliation... iron fists as outlaws who gained higher education...I know a gladiator... their ancestors where whipped, beaten, degraded, emasculated...treated as property...used...sold...and traded...yet...they made it...populated making the battlefields packed with warriors to fight some of the biggest battles...of the mind...engaging in the fight ...the controversy...public arena the worldly stereotypes...released and free...finding the fight for land, bread, housing, intelligence, clothing, justice and peace... I salute them greatly...I know a gladiator...he may have not walked across the stage at the end of 12th grade....but he sewed together his trades...to empower and show perseverance to his babies...I know a gladiator...who is more than a daddy...and never takes a day off the grind so he can uplift his family's life with every dime...I know a gladiator...who demands respect...and wouldn't settle for a life in a set founded by black panther rejects...I know a gladiator...not a thug, a hood nigga, morally unrestrained...but determined, sterling, admirable, and well trained...I know a gladiator...not a panderer, vermin, defiler, uprooted or pained...but deluxe, superior, reputable, first class men...I know a gladiator...life could have been without struggle...or some bumps and bruises that caused trouble...yet survived it...and the show isn't over but they haven't left doors open for a continual look over the shoulder...I know a gladiator...if he knows himself too there will never be a time where is found in the position of a stoop...he stands tall and proud...not compromising self-worth being loud, crass, and vile...but a gentleman in the face of adversity...not prideful of knuckling up to settle disputes because quiet as it's kept he's too worthy...I know a gladiator beating ignorance and blasphemy...circulating uplifting examples in the core city streets of Cincinnati...I know a gladiator...with ambitions of not settling scores and signed over his life to potentially end up as a prisoner of war...I know a gladiator...burned through stripes like flames and will do anything for you...boots have roots that can be traced back to Columbus GA...I know a gladiator...he could easily seek pity...young and black in the inner city of the windy city...iron lung...sturdy shell...remarkable sparkle in his eyes as he is compelled to not let he or his loved ones get derailed...I know a gladiator... he is my father...my grandfathers ...my uncles...my brothers...my nephews...my cousins...my dear male friends....my sons.....my man....see a gladiator risks legal and social standing equation the everyday life of a male black American...appearing in a similar ancient Coliseum in Rome...socially marginalized with harsh conditions at school and home...with no choice...forced into this stadium the day he was born...being the minority...even the tiniest inclination to defend self-preservation which sometimes garnished popular acclaim and admiration...I know a gladiator...he spends every day finding a new way to get down the streets that are already paved...he's inventive...not looking to see what he can get from society...always looking to see what he can give back...his armor protects him from potential blasts of catastrophe in the size of the Titans...he's honest...trustworthy...loyal...and kind...because he knows the universe with its karma is color blind...I know a gladiator...I never felt something so strong and true...I am blessed to know and love such gladiators...I hope you know and love one too.....

Snow Angels in June

Her eyes...were watching GOD...making snow angels in June watching balloons drift to the moon...innocence...still intact...life forms while a life forms to enjoy the minimal things that make her smile as she is accepted to the world...her eyes were watching GOD...as the earth sways and bends...bend my heart back with the weight of doubt and grief. And bundles of Joi...planting bonsais...screaming bonsai while my pupils gather salt rain then stream down my cheekbones slowly... I must admit my eyes were too watching GOD... but my sins make me turn away and she saw promise in his cornea so she decided to stay...engulfed in the stare between her and the entity who whisk, blended, and poured, and molded her to be...to be more than just a space indented with her anatomy...more than posing for the photo-lens blowing raspberries....more than just that dimple on her chin...she left notes...in my uterus for the future fetus so they were aware of her soul...at birth... her finger prints on my ribcage more than adequate DNA...I never knew love like this...I watched...as her eyes were watching GOD...as it went from every blue moon to every blue sky...continual...constant...I wondered why...now her wings attached to her backbone hard as a steel rod unlike mine cause she could watch GOD and her purity and innocence made her recognize the promise...the security ... the peace deep within the muscle of her flesh her wings...angelic...silk threads...feathered tails...plucked one from the middle and dipped in the North Atlantic to feed the blue whales... she's the epitome to me...she left a familiar place to lay in foreign arms which she had seen before being conceived...so brave...and content...before the final rest in man's world I know for a fact...her eyes were watching GOD...

Pretty Girl Rock

Don't hate me because I'm beautiful...hate me because I'm BOLD...hate me because my mind has the capacity to look for hidden motivational messages in some of the deepest tragedies...don't hate me because I'm beautiful...hate me because of my grace through the monstrous bombs that hide in current space then twist and turn and explode in my face...I'm still here...hate me because no matter how tattered and shattered I should be by those with wicked intent can't manipulate my existence or sabotage my awesome gifts...don't hate...me...because I'm beautiful, hate me because my faith remains unmovable and my heart sterile...I don't mind being the woman I am...don't hate me because I'm beautiful...that's silly... childish and useless...you think I would rather be beautiful but yet clueless...? hate me because of the wealth of knowledge that dwells in my shell, hate me because my confidence is remarkable and no matter how onyx my eyes are they still sparkle...and my laugh defends flames from rainforests and keeps Niagara Falls glistening in beauty...and humorous just don't encompass my arms cause I can make you laugh uncontrollably... if you need it...hate me because courage, tranquility, serenity, love, bravery, articulation and intelligence has solidified in my spine and delightfully settled in my blood and stimulated my mind...don't hate me because I smile and break bread with those who have tried to condemn my soul to mediocrity...don't hate...embrace the caliber of individual I am and beauty is only skin deep so don't focus this gorgeous face...there's more to me...and if you take the time to accept this truth and get to know me...you won't hate me at all

HER

I look for her and then she is me....I live for
her...she lives through me....unlike uncharted
philosophies she's the
greatest...incomprehensible as challenging
arithmetic...she resembles strength...her brain
cells would be an example of a phenomenon of
the mind...her characteristics ring "sheroic"...she
builds empires with sapphires a beast like statute
with inner victories....I look her...she finds
me...so envision dandelions...
sunflowers...cotton....cotton that pricked the
terminals of her hands causing broken skin and
infection...the same fingers that soothed babies
close to perfection...the ones that motioned to an
individual in sternness or affection...or the ones
bonded behind her back while the slave master
prepared his erection...and the process with
perception leaves immaculate theory for
rejection...but don't reject her...she cultivates the
virtues...strength and dignity are her clothing,
and she smiles at the future poised she opens her
mouth in wisdom, teaching of kindness is on her
tongue, charm is deceitful and beauty is vain, but
a woman who fears the LORD, she shall be
praised... GOD makes her so uncomfortable that

she will do the very thing she fears...her beauty like Nefertiti, the bottom of her feet bruised with callus...discernment is resilient as it attacks her spirit...give her a second...she won't fail...on the edge of meaningless compliance...she prayed...she swayed to negro spirituals...she remained brave...she wept only by herself during supplication...she embodies the sound vessel...at a level that the man who lacerated her backside...couldn't understand why she never cried...damnit I look for her... and she finds me...through striking resemblance it is certain we belong in the same family tree...I look for her...when society is asking why am I so eager to unleash my capabilities...I look for her...when submission feels like the bitter end of my own individual existence and my legs are so sore from trudging through indigent excuses...I search for her...in the roots of my kinky hair and the retina of my onyx eyes I am her...settled with my impurity because a victorious day comes to light with clarity... I look for her...as one would search the Kimberlites of South Africa to find that one diamond with no blemish...I look for her...in my dreams...I look for her...through my tears...I look for her...through my hurt...I look for her...to understand...I look for her to calm my fears...I look for her to embrace simplicity and happiness that reeks truth...I look for her because she keeps me close to HIM...

Stones

Universally prone to harvest stones of wisdom...this young black woman will solemnly bring testimony...when it comes to what is best for me and my seeds it's no democracy...it's a dictatorship, I am the law of my life...I have to be...I look at the strength in Ethel Smith and know why the city of Cincinnati named a day for her...I recall Carrie Holmes and know why my belief in Christ is so strong...I close my eyes and visualize Verdis Blair and Willa Ruth Hall and Susie Pullins, I smile with great gratitude cause real talk, I have it all.... from my bloodline and the distant time line...the woman of color built to last, built to stand, hard to fall and when you ask how strong...too strong...when you ask how smart...too smart...that's how the cells got tinted with the colors of the rainbow...we are irresistible that's why since 1655 slave masters were sniffing for them brown hides...

The melanin caressing deep in our skin, the lips that curve and plump, the hips spread prepared to let life leave our canal, and a heart of integrity, platinum covered...universally prone to harvest stones of wisdom..."

"Nobody ever helps me into carriages, or over mud-puddles, or gives me any best place! And ain't I a woman? Look at me! Look at my arm! I have ploughed and planted, and gathered into barns, and no man could head me! And ain't I a woman? I could work as much and eat as much as a man - when I could get it - and bear the lash as well! And ain't I a woman? I have borne thirteen children, and seen most all sold off to slavery, and when I cried out with my mother's grief, none but Jesus heard me! And ain't I a woman?" - Sojourner Truth delivered these words-1851... after reading this I wonder these days how any black woman could EVER attempt to doubt herself...

Harriet Tubman carried that revolver and threatened to shoot even men who had grown scared and impaired from the long journey towards freedom...the Most High spoke through her injury and gave her needed premonition that helped lead thousands of slaves off the plantation, singlehandedly...chosen...Moses...pioneer to unrestraint...not a man...a black woman...confident in the voice of GOD...as he spoke directly to her soul...sustained in her heels... fused in her knees...where she prayed diligently for release... can't no one argue with that...universally prone to harvest stones of wisdom...

Salty, jazz-hued vocals...when being black was a crime and she could have passed for white or Hispanic...she said "nah...I won't separate from my African-American DNA...I won't come to Hollywood and play your maid"...not with this voice... that ascends...and transcends and sends hope...and when she made it...not having to walk through the back door anymore...head held high...beautiful, sultry, immaculate smile, flawless skin, honor as she main stayed Civil Rights, March on Washington...put a hand in the passing of Anti-lynching laws...obviously put here for more than one cause....4 Grammy's, and seven other plaques of prestige to include the NAACP image award...a star the day she was born...I can't look in the mirror without seeing Lena Horne...black woman...endured whatever...out lived whatever...brought meaning to fusion of black and white......she stuck with black...knowing of the adversity...knowing the non-acceptance...no shame in it...universally prone to harvest stones of wisdom...

As she watched her a great man, her husband, best friend...get gunned down...as she carried youth in her womb...nightmares plagued her eyes...even when she was awake...the awful smell of the gun smoke that wrenched her everyday...and she went on a pilgrimage to the place that set her mate free...regained her way...regained the faith to give it to her offspring and their offspring too, as she traveled the states with her council for black women...coalition for youths to have beneficial learning...if I ever would have met her I would have greeted her with applause...universally prone to harvest stones of wisdom Mrs. Betty Shabazz...

The test comes with stressed faith...and ascends higher than we can reach...but I carry the weight and desire to reach anyway...When I tilt to the mirror the reflection I have becomes so clear...I stand proud as I see Coretta Scott King, Marian Anderson, Billie Holliday, Hattie McDaniel, Dorothy Dandridge- the spirits of these souls capturing me day to day....then the liveliness of Phylicia Rashad, Etta James, Michelle Obama, Maya Angelou, And I now know why the caged bird sings, being entrapped in the realm of faint reality, but the mere fantasy just because life isn't what it should be, it never was...but these women show me how to persevere... and I am amazing, homerun hitter, never afraid of being awesome and I'm not a quitter...I don't fear that I am powerful beyond measure...I love that beyond measure, I'm powerful...from my lineage, from my race, from my GOD...from Carin Suzette Hall...my beautiful, strong, smart mother...and her mother...my " Big Mom" never leaving any room for doubt...self-sufficient, magnificent, articulate, independent...and universally prone to harvest stones of wisdom

Helen of Troy

My soul strong to the magnitude that's unreachable, my sturdy back and shoulders that carries the weight and the hate of the word...my diversity to withstand adversity is something that my ancestry wilted into the marrow that's deep within my bones,

Unacceptable is what I think I reach for faith and the people I encounter shun thought of doing the right thing...it's times like this that I wish I could sing-high notes to pour out the sorrow and condolences to the many that I pray for that will never acknowledge their worth...as GOD creeps into the crevice of my flesh, I find myself depressed because sometimes I can't help cursing...I can't help but wonder why the anointed won't anoint so that the message is spread the way it's supposed to at its best and you and me evangelist...like our duty to work and pay taxes...and the government repays with that fat check...but with tithes we blessed with heaven sent...coils of mercy and please don't misunderstand...I'm not sitting in a pew every time I get a chance, because I can be in my kitchen and feel his presence so I dance, I see the innocence in my kid's eyes and despise myself because I feel I'm not truly giving them a chance....

My soul so strong to the magnitude that stretches past the stars to test the matter of the air, my calf muscles with slight definition from trying to jump up there...from kicking away childish, not needed attention because as I failed to mention the man himself has been tested...but I rest at night...thinking of how I can change the world the next day but I can't...I can only be the change I would like to see....busted through the barricades with escalades of authority I own my destiny...compliments of GOD for protecting my faith...

The tension that is built up in my temples causes blurred vision from eye sight...thank GOD he let me also see through my heart...so I can love...so I can be...so I can perform beyond measure to the mounds of intelligence in this subject I'm subject to snap cause I'm tired of seeing minor people get major airplay and take for granted the afforded opportunities wondering only what's it in for them...never persecuting the individual but looking sideways at the act...that's how you move past the injustice that has hit your heart with heavy impact

So matter fact real talk this is where it's at , when that judgment day comes and I'm standing before him I am going to be weak, worn, torn, tired, pressed, stressed, sleepy, quiet, with my arms outstretched to show GOD that I used all of my skeletal, intellectual, spirits and gifts he blessed me with....that I didn't waste a moment judging who didn't walk on water...that I loved both my parents...they loved each other enough to mix DNA for me...nothing else even matters...that I spoke kind words when they could have been harsh, that I love hard and didn't care about clothes, money, and cars...that I was patient with the ones I adore and the ones who rubbed me the wrong way...yet I'm human so I have to be mindful here on earth so I can party with my fallen relatives and my 6 month old baby girl behind the gates who has passed away

My soul so strong that when it appears weak I am glad because I see the true characters of those that surround me...for we are measured by how we treat the man of low substance than the one with brains and power... these random thoughts capture me and I only can express them when an barrel full of ink finds me...and I share...I have to...it's a must...part of the mission to reinstate what is not only lost in the world but also in me...buried...until I cry...to the point my eyes swell and I need water to hydrate the pores only to cry again...and again...troubled...but never confused...defused sometimes...blind...dwelling in that crab cancer shell wishing for true unity...between you and me...her and him...selfishness abolished as it can be considered an "US" –my soul is so strong because that's the way GOD made me.

Tell Him

You are truly rare to your breed but yet you make it relevant why your kind exists...the electric energy that passes through each ventricle and atrium of my heart when we kiss...but you wouldn't believe it...it's cool...you don't have too...Sean john should try an experiment on your body's chemistry so he can change his fragrance "unforgettable" to what you transform it to...

Your touch is therapeutic...potent and lucid...and we are bonded for life...through fire and wind...you were designed and perfected to be connected and reflected through me and me through you ...and when I created this piece on a bonded slice of tree I realized the joy and love that you bring...it's like I am looking at music...it's like I'm looking at potential lyrics of a song gone platinum
I tell you when you I am mad...I cry when I'm sad...and I say go away...leave me alone...but not today...today I'm rebelling...as I'm inspired by the miseducation of Lauryn Hill...cause she said "tell him" So I will...at night I like your chocolate arms to wrap around me while I sleep because if the Lord don't let me wake...at least...your flesh was

the last warm blanket I felt...

Although the nature or essence of love is a subject of frequent debate, I say love is power...and gripping like a controlled substance...addictive and may sometimes cause delusions...so yes it's been confirmed you and I are crazy....

The indication as I fell my brain was steady releasing pheromones, dopamine, and serotonin to name a few chemicals that ran through my cerebral and never left... enzymes manifested in my nervous system for two thousand, three hundred, and ten days...and counting....passion applied to the admiration that I have for you.... For putting up with me...but I put up with you even when it seems like you trip on every full moon...but how often are those? 12 times a year- 72 times in 6 years- which leaves two thousand, two hundred, and thirty eight times that you are waxing and waning, while I'm squirming and singing in the melody of the sweetest thing;) the secretion of words barely uttered from my throat...my knees weak...knock faintly as the best moment which happens again and again and again...and then I feel like I'm running through a field of lilies and lilacs, and the sun is barely setting...and the air is not too crisp but just right and then I am brought back to life in your arms, warm, gentle...hands that have learned to tame themselves to find the necessary part of my anatomy to soothe...42 Beats per minute your heart pulsating...wait a minute 84 beats per minute because now our heart shares the same drum...that's why I married you....because emotionally, physically, and mentally I will go through every motion with you....

You are truly part of a rare breed but yet you make it relevant why your kind exists... to lift...to cultivate...celebrate...to learn, grow and succeed as a young man first to conquer as a King last...I promise your breed confuses me....but then I look at you and know why your kind exists....

Census

I'm watching...amused yet angered...leaving a piece of my heart on that plantation...those who knew me said I was strong...said I was classy...said I was brave...my momma always told me my courage would someday lead to my demise...and surprise...momma knows best...one brother was the quiet one...my other brother stubborn...my daddy dead...struck twice to his head before master took my momma to the shed...I had a baby sister...with ocean blue eyes...and curls the size of nickels in her hair...her skin not quite as muddy as mind...but fair...last time I saw her she was 5...the world wasn't so gracious to me but something told me she would be fine...I'm watching...over the decades I could show up in the wind and I saw slavery end...I saw the women of my roots and the same color as my skin shopping with they own wallets and writing with their own pens...I'm watching...evolution...I'm watching...a solution...I'm watching...mind pollution...I'm watching enslavement of a mentality that fights against normalcy...parts of society that has embraced educational vibrancy as the white man's property...when NO...cause I was a white man's property and believe me...it's not the same...I'm watching...I was relieved when he would take a break from the stick...and made another slave crack me with that whip...but now....who is calling the shots? Who is handing over the lashes? I'm watching...I'm waiting...I'm wanting...to see the strong, the classy, the brave who are living with free will and not a slave...I'm watching to see who wants to own the security of not living up to what society has said you have to be....I'm watching to see the worth....because being driven with that rod from an iron fist made me jerk...and 400 years later I'm watching the same movements but it's referred to as a twerk....I'm watching...sometimes flustered...cause Willie Lynch called it....when we all thought at that time he was bluffing...ain't that something...I'm watching...not the celebrities cause they have enough eyes...not the pioneers cause of the blood, sweat, and tears were wrenched from their soul for the prize...not the abolitionist, liberal and civil right activists, I'm watching those who will fill out a form for census...I'm watching ….

Exiled

Put down... tossed away into a corner...dust and mites collected on on my bridges of stability designed for you... every time your limbs inserted into my root I gave you hope for what you would had never seen... you stood toe to toe in opposition with me... I treated your body like my own... protecting your extremities from hot coal when you danced with the devil at times...I grew wings below the platform so you could close your eyes and reach God hands out to touch the omnipotent with divine simplicity... I took you the furthest because I never saved any energy for the voyage back... your whole existence equipped and consist of the mass of luminous sphere of plasma held together by gravity most prominently on the celestial domain grouped together into constellations and asterisms...you shine due to the thermal nuclear attention of hydrogen into helium... in your core... my star...no matter where you were going I was up for it... no matter when you returned I was never tired... since 1000 B.C. my components more permanently join to form a single unit... insulated to keep you elevated now no longer entrusted...exiled... but I was there...there when you lifted your warm, limp baby in your arms and pressed your mouth against her milk stained lips to transfer air from your lungs to hers...tired with the authorities I held all your weight... I heard you whimper in the night confused and diffused and at your bedside I wouldn't dare let there be another pair of shoes you needed me...to stand and salute...as your full bird Colonel and major showed up to your front door in uniform... people often asked was I issued for the BDUs or for personal use I pointed you the other way... lackadaisical right face because our relationship was far too complex to be explained to the next in tuned me and you... we met two days after your moms and pops cried as you left and you never wept until your Nana left and we made it through that together... I carried you.. I never let you surrender... I never let you fall... I never let your soles perspire to the point of needing Scholls...while individuals stared down their noses to find flaws in you... but never the way you stood... never the way you looked...chin up I had you...I marched your lil feisty ass up to the putrid souls that attempted to condemn your existence to mediocrity and let them know under no circumstance would you be forced to be the individual with no voice so kick rocks! I gave you strength beyond measure I maintained your image as that short young black woman that grip stability foot protection suitable to a rugged environment is me... I held you when you started to trudge... and I gripped your ankle when you needed a hug... but now I'm put down tossed away into a corner...dust and mites collected on my bridges of stability...designed...for you...

Indigo's Bluez

Let's see what you can say to me...back and forth...no mystery...I know your calligraphy can entrap me like whoa...but as I arch and point... will you have any words besides how good it feels...no blurred lines...I dropped the v-laced cloth which covered my grail...not holy...cause I have spoiled...like 5 times...when I eliminate the secretions that have been brewing...Heineken feel in your thrusts you don't even trust what may come when you let go...I need at least a fragment though...eminence tells me that you have a set of eyes that I haven't fell into yet...because I would purposely let you smash from the......I don't want to see that milky way dynasty...I lost to win...but really...I want a mental boost....boost me to greatness...boost me to love you...boost me to wet these sheets like a 4 yr. old after a bad dream...smash to boost loose the tight wet tunnel...cake it...funnel the flow...but nigga you betta at least put up a fight...you betta boost to shut me up...do you need a boost until its implied "you won"...needing enrichment from your "man print" is the outcome...I tried to boost you and move you a little to the left because the tunnel's damn will break again...leaving you in a motion for stroking but no words...worth listening to...though my mind moves in the depths as previously debreed scar tissue hurts with the pain of a thousand itches which can't scratched or flickered...our salvation is the remedy...calamine like can I mind you when we out these sheets....in the streets...when we in the booth....and it's like 65 degrees...waiting 17 seconds for the drop...can you at least give me 4 bars...I can drop warm minutes from my time clock...yet still have blood to circulate as my heart pumps therefore visual art still sprays...never been intrigued to know what it feels like to enter a world entrapped by foreplay of wordplay...unimaginable ways of touching that part of my soul...awakened...deep...where I want you to dwell and teach me...shut me up...tell me something in the way you manipulate my skin...that I win...all of you...

Cincinnati

My home....landmark of controversy...yet in still my home....Cincinnati....where my ancestors relocated to during the trials of slavery...the duplex home on Trimble and the one level brick on Yarmouth...the train tracks by Peabody...and Monning....places where we pulled up there was love...to see my twigs of the family oak spoke volumes, those butterflies that filled up my belly, especially on Christmas in Blue Ash...that phone call of excitement that my Aunt was on break from college in Atlanta and now home and my cousin made it safe from DC, or my Uncle that just had a new baby...the great Aunt who has beat breast cancer all accessible and free...the siblings that mean the world to me, when I think of these things, I look where it all began for me...Cincinnati

Where Jazz fest rings, Taste of Cincinnati is off the chain, the Black Family Reunion or a day at Kings Island...and of course the name brands that you can't live without you will find there, from Vendors, to Barqs red crème soda, and those Grippos...and I know to someone who is not a native would not give a damn...cause in the newspapers and CNN...Cincinnati is slammed...banned for the adversity

Like we are the only place with racist cops and crooked city officials...or the drug cartel is so ginormous that it's a common pressed issue with this small city where you can get anywhere there no matter where you at in 15 minutes...don't get me wrong it does break my heart that I have high school friends that have committed suicide or gunned down in front of their homes, that 2 year olds are molested and then murdered, where my twenty year old cousin was killed on his birthday, police brutality, acquittal of a racist cop that sparked the curfew that even my 70 year grandfather had to abide to...I could hang my head low and curse the place I was born and raised...but I can't...it's my home...Cincinnati

Where on June 30th at 5:47 in the evening at Good Samaritan I came in this world, where my daddy joined the union of boilermakers, where my mother exceeded solo driving city buses known as metro...where my brother played football and wrestled upholding our school mascot- The Trojan...where my sister kept her mind in them books while playing every sport...implanted and intertwined in the ground strong rooted all around...sometimes I wish I would have stayed...

Cincinnati...downtown Cincinnati...I used to drive over to the skyline at Mt Adams and wonder where my life would take me...that was a time I didn't have to worry if someone was lurking in the woods to rape me...cause everyone knows everyone...relatives in every hood and even when you thought you were alone and no one saw you... they did...where the girls' nails and hair stay fly...and Carla's' and Smitty's stayed packed...the pre-holiday at golden skates...the strip after Eden park...but then....the riots... not surprised if a black man is killed holding a fork to twenty white police officers armed with nines...where the love for money so potent that even the smartest black boys fell victim...senseless...yet it doesn't shame me...because I have done nothing in my power to go back and change it!

I hear there are street cars soon to show their face, road improvements...yeah finally supposedly Martin Luther's King's street will have a pleasantly sightful place...the neighborhood enhancement project...I'm waiting to see and hear of the effects...cause I so for real LOVE my city...I love the Bearcats and the Bengals, I love the Reds, I love my alma mater...I love my family and friends that are doing their thing maintaining to this day...I'm the ONLY chick in San Antonio clubs doing the down-the way... I know there are elements to Cincinnati that aren't pleasing...but I see my people strive and the hope to impact positively one day lets me sleep at night...where hopefully the hoods aren't trenches but castles...where the black community has a country club...with soul food on the menu...where the suggestion won't be made to build walls around the projects to" protect the wealthy", where the healthcare reform will ensure a chance for all our babies to be born healthy...where that desolate land on 75 becomes alive...all of this vibe from a beautiful picture of my city at night yesterday I saw on line...duty calls by Uncle Sam for now...but in due time I am going to return to the city I love most...Cincinnati...

Thank You for Your Support

I hope you enjoyed my poetry. In the coming months, I will be releasing a audio CD of my spoken word.

Please take a moment to like my FB page: "SHE"

Your can view my live spoken word performances on YouTube under the name Stacy Wylie.

To book a live performance please email me at poeticprodigy81@live.com

Love & Peace

Stacy Wylie